Talking to Trees

through poetry and pictures

Talking to Trees

through poetry and pictures

B Sedgwick

Spirit Moxie
www.spiritmoxie.com
2022

© 2022 by Sally B Sedgwick

All rights reserved.

See The Forest of Support for a list of images used with permission.

ISBN: 978-1-7338642-4-4
e-ISBN: 978-1-7338642-3-7

Library of Congress Control Number: 2021922774

Cover and Interior Design: Lynne Hudson
Cover Photo: Matthew Collins

Published by Spirit Moxie
www.spiritmoxie.com
Portland, Oregon

In honor of trees, but especially in memory of the old cherry tree which produced beautiful white cherries and grew outside my bedroom window when I was a teenager. One day, as I watched from my window, our little dog streaked by and out of its way as the tree slowly toppled over in full bloom.

"I never saw a discontented tree. They grip the ground as though they liked it, and though fast rooted they travel about as fast as we do."

— John Muir

Table of Contents

Preface	11
Poems and Pictures	13
The Tree Who Asked to be a Poem	14
House Corner	16
Archetype	18
Photo Op	20
Connections	22
Interconnection	24
Isolation	26
Being	28
Green and Aubergine	30
Companions	32
Driveway Denizen	34
Skeleton or …	36
Twins	38
Phoenix	40
Seduction	42
Photo Bombs	44
Shock	46
Identity	48
Promises	50
Spring Visit	52
So Beautiful	54
Forgotten Phone	56

Poems without Pictures	59
April Snow	61
Passing By	63
Not Even Video...	65
Pictures without Poems	67
The Forest of Support	83
About the Author	85

Preface

As soon as it was published (December 2011), I found myself reading Martha Beck's *Finding Your Way in a Wild New World*. One of the experiences she describes is attending an ayahuasca ceremony, where she participated without actually taking any of the drug. (Why not was based on a possible life threatening interaction with a prescribed pill she'd taken shortly before.) But she was still part of the the ceremony's shamanic circle. During the session she experiences the trees singing to her. I wanted that! It sounded real, connected, and life giving.

Shortly after reading about this experience, I took a long, solo drive to a wedding in North Carolina, leaving behind my partner who was trying, and failing, to recover from multiple surgeries and complications. On my drive, I could sense the beautiful trees lining the highway calling out love and support.

To be fair, I've later "heard" trees asking for care and lamenting their own disease. Nonetheless, this began my love affair with trees as conversations.

While I read, and enjoyed, the more scientific words of Peter Wohlleben's *The Hidden Life of Trees*, it has been watching and interacting with actual trees during the past two years that has resulted in this book. It began when I was unexpectedly included in a writer's group in Bangkok during an exploration of "do I want to live here?" (The answer was "not now.") We were given the prompt of writing from the point of view of an object. Intrigued by the prompt, somehow a tree that blocked the sidewalk between me and the grocery store demanded to be the subject of a poem, but not the speaker. And so these poems began.

So come with me. Trees talk. Their voices have gotten louder, more supportive, more individual as I've been writing. I invite you to listen too.

Poems
and
Pictures

The Tree Who Asked to be a Poem

They say we're related

Atoms, stardust

But haunted? Omnipotent?

You break sidewalks

Dare us to tread on you

March in a row

Guard the temple wall

Guide my path to market

And always I see you in other trees

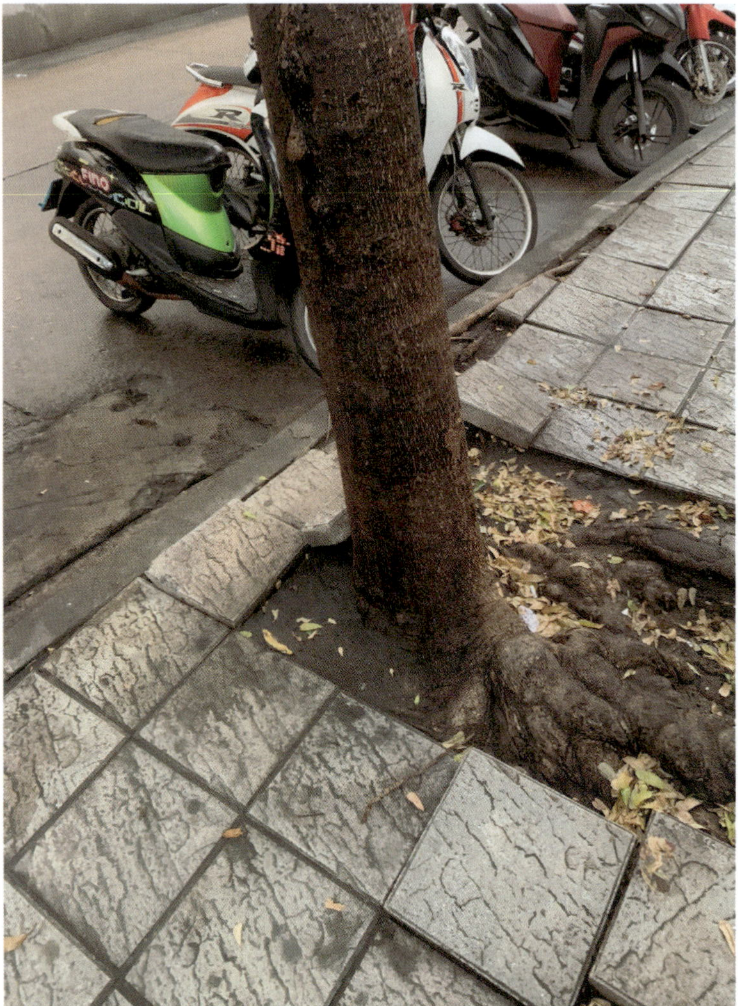

House Corner

First you were raccoons in the walls.
Or squirrels

But

Noise by my bed became branches
    brushing, beating
    blowing

Wind friend, solace

I mourn your trimming
 in a more silent room

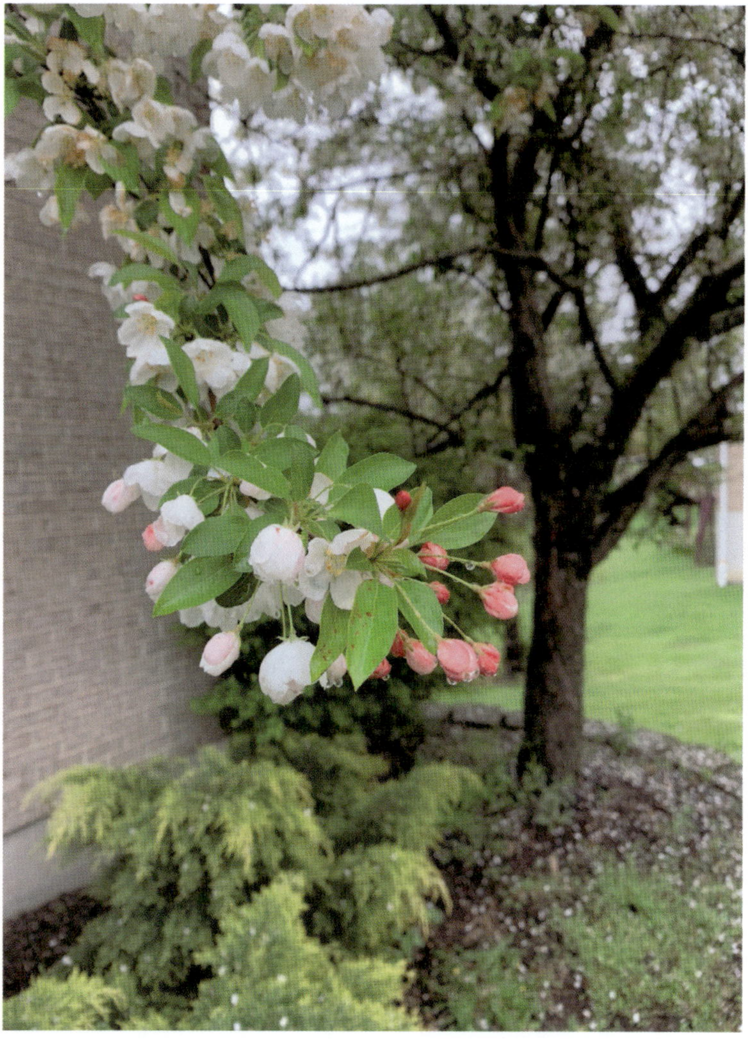

Archetype

Three people
A simple longish ride
Indiana countryside

Look! A perfect tree!
A coloring book drawing
Symmetrical
Round

One person couldn't see

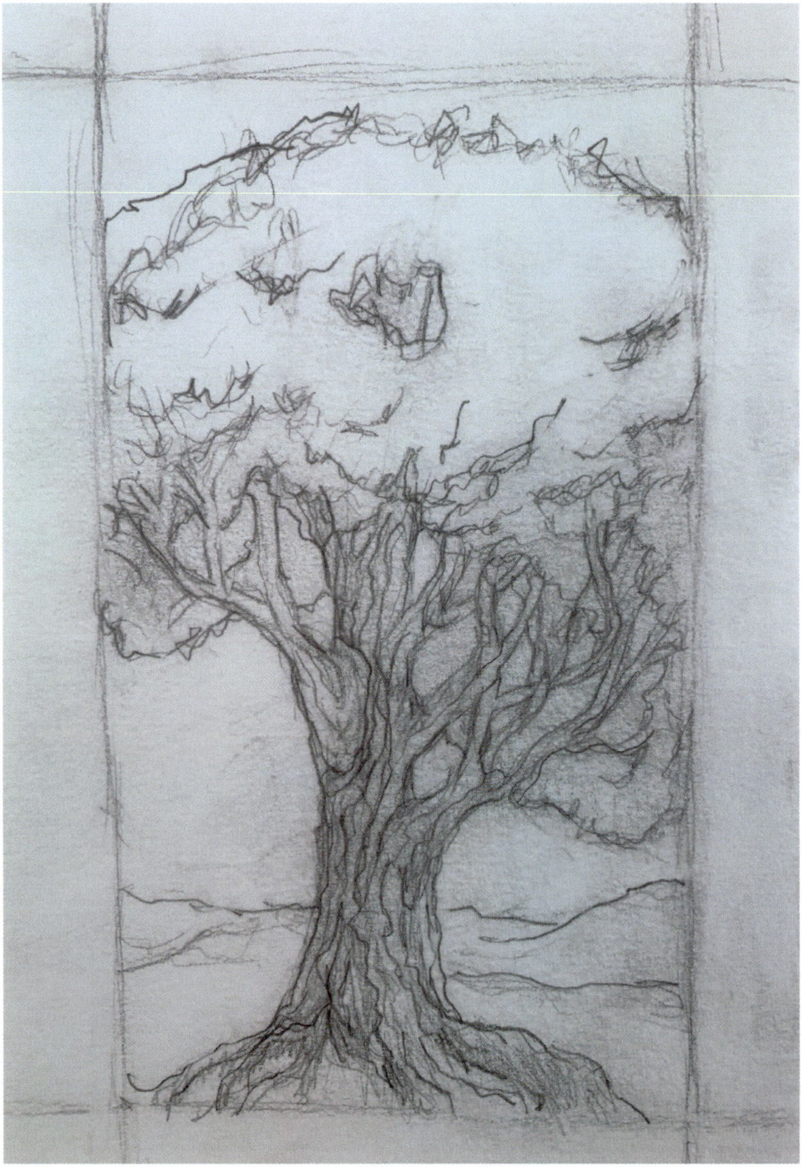

Photo Op

Pick me,
 pick me!

Children jumping
Diva's primping

Tiny, majestic
 gnarled
 svelte

Wild, trimmed

The trees toss in the wind

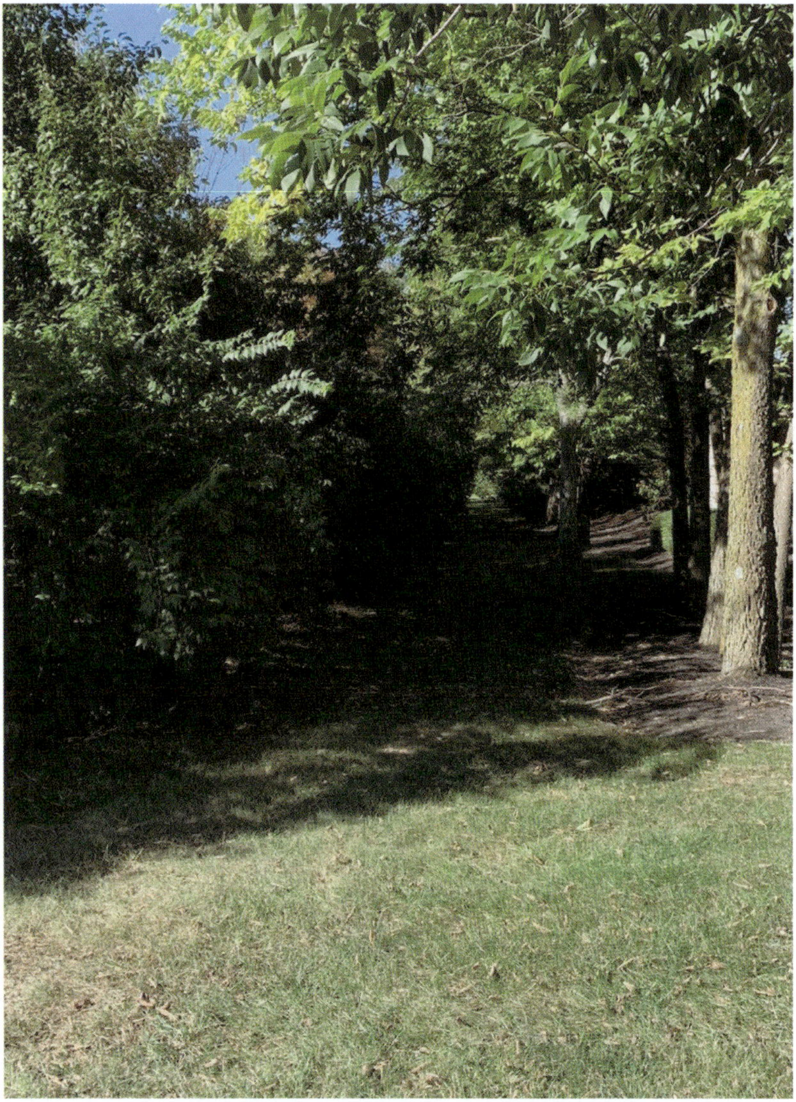

Connections

In the photo it looks tall–
  Not old or large

But heart leaping I heard
A storm
And you
Running to hug it. "Hang on!"

Naming it
Mother for us all

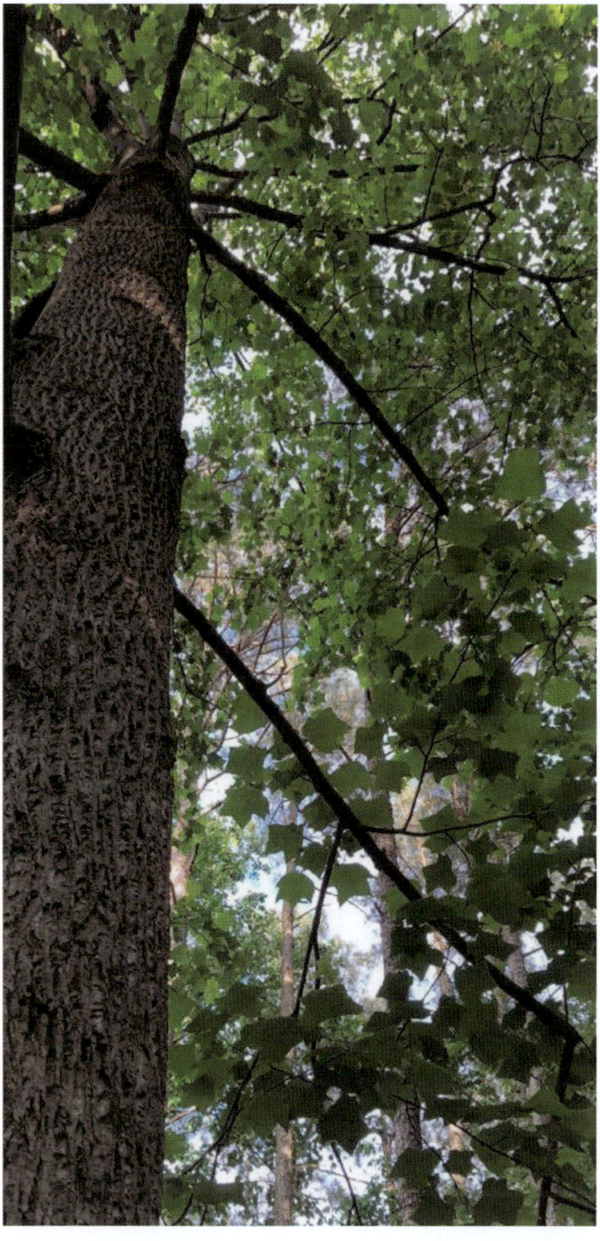

Interconnection

"Pull a card," I said. "Sure, an herbal card."

A tree!

Roots spreading

Branches waving

Protecting

Reaching

But needing water

And more water

To keep the tendrils whole

WILLOW - INTERCONNECTION

Isolation

Isolation

A current norm

Yet every time I sit, drink in hand,
 confronting loneliness

You reach

Murmur

Are just there

I can't explain how or why

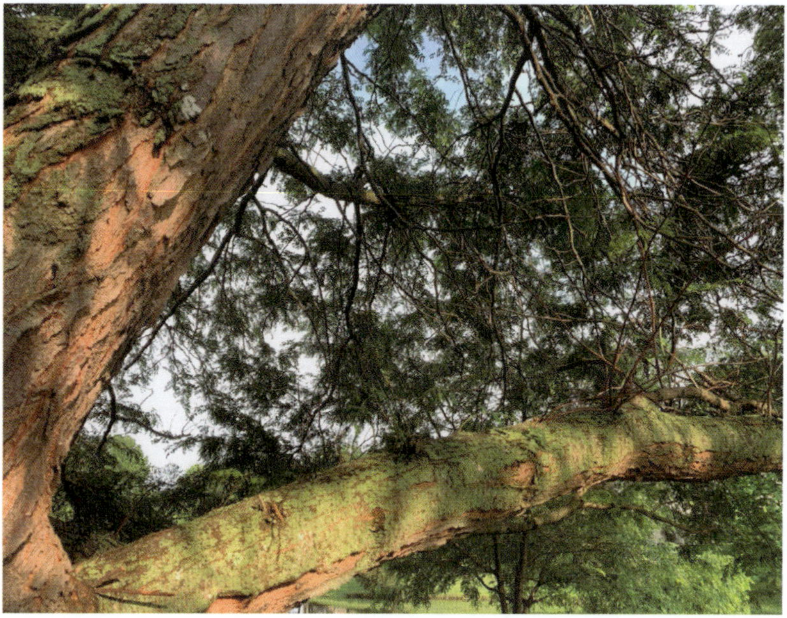

Being

So beautiful
  waiting for Spring
  perfect now

Complete

No yearn for
  Taller
  Fuller
  Landscape
  Even leaves

May I be so whole

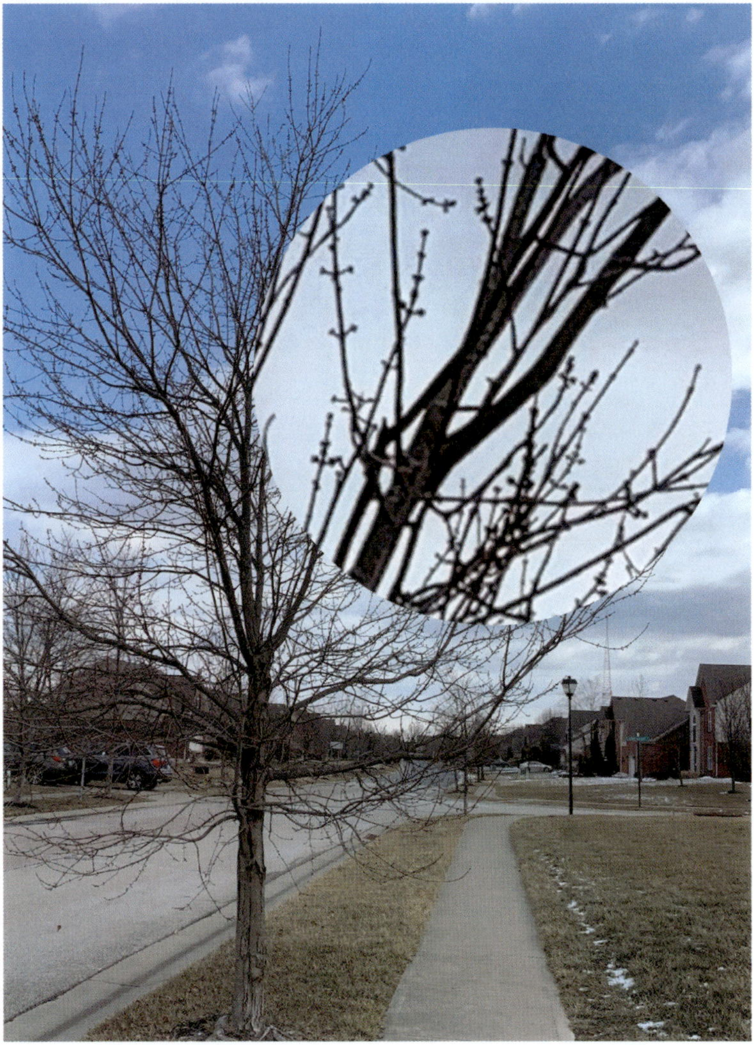

Green and Aubergine

Photosynthesis

such a big word.

junior high science extolling green

Yet

Here you are - mixed neighbors

both, apparently, exuding

Oxygen

Where did purple learn to transform the sun?

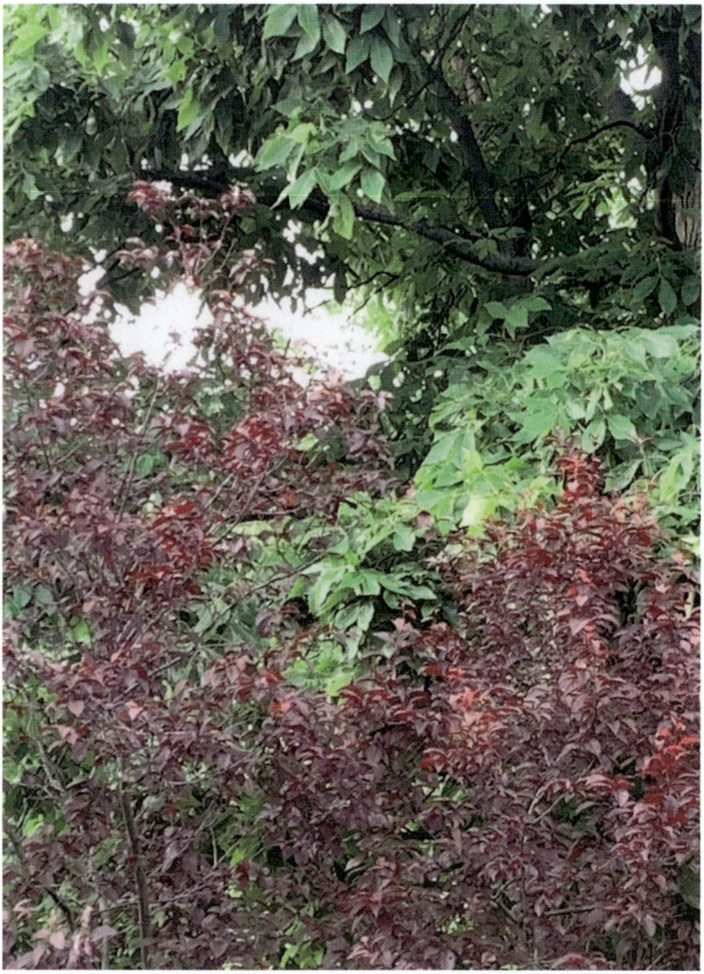

Companions

Companions are useful

Odd discussions

Walking partners

Missing?

Today I was full:

Ideas, rhythm,

Possibility

Vision

And alone

When the trees beckoned

"We're here!"

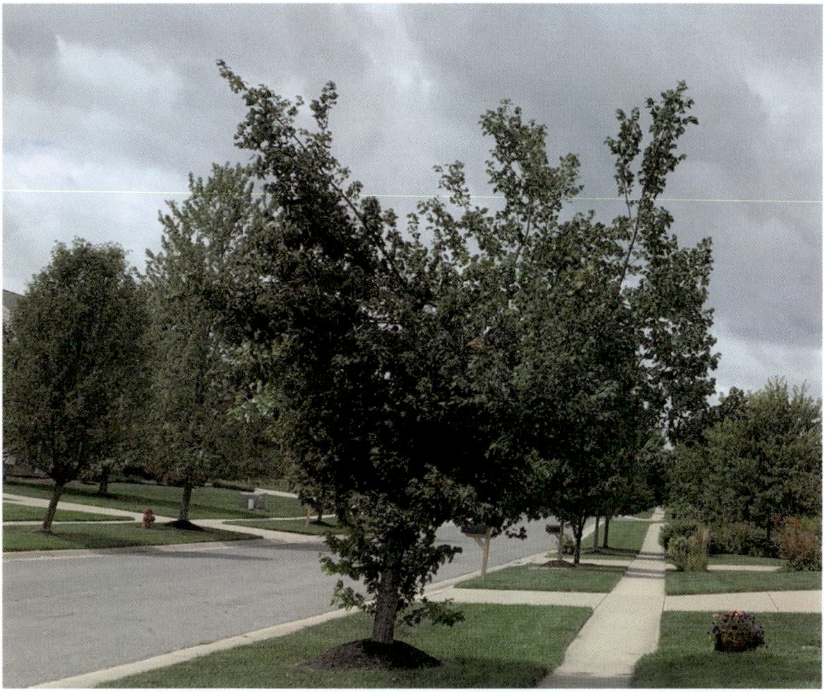

Driveway Denizen

Slanting Curving Silent

You mark with grace – or maybe trauma

What shaped you?

Light

 Wind

 Possibility

Silly fears worry you'll fall

They could see

Strength

 Grace

 God

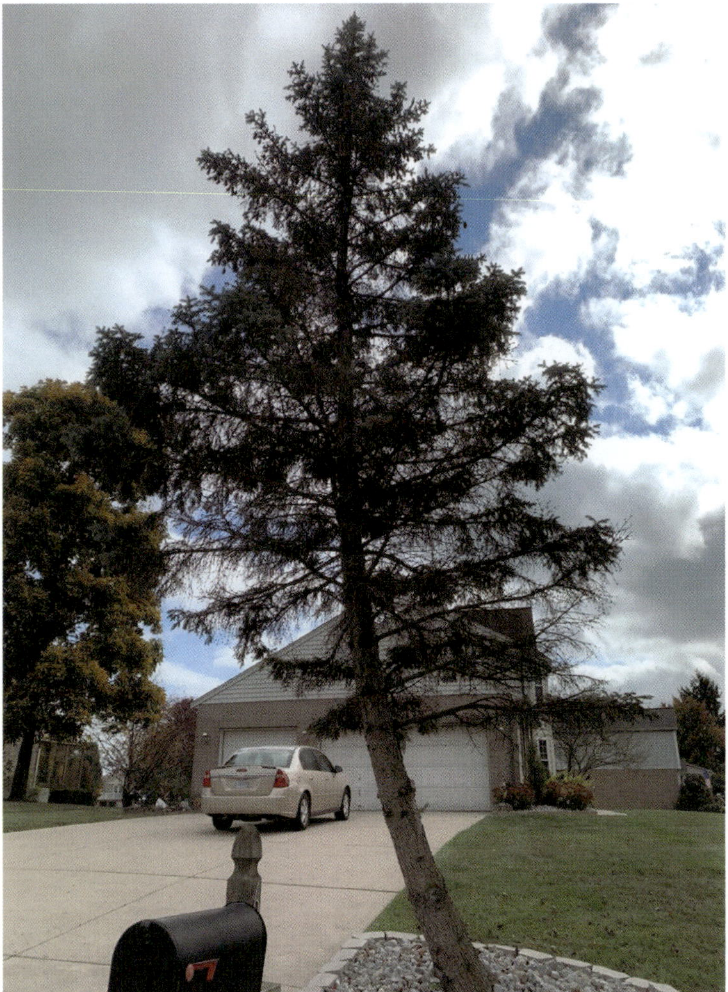

Skeleton or ...

Skeletons - boring, boney,
Predictable
  to an untrained eye

Unlike nudes,
  clothed in membrane
Marked by age, care, neglect

As nude, you're
  a winter of tangles and lines
Intimate, interesting, reaching
Unapologetic

Beautiful without summer's clothes

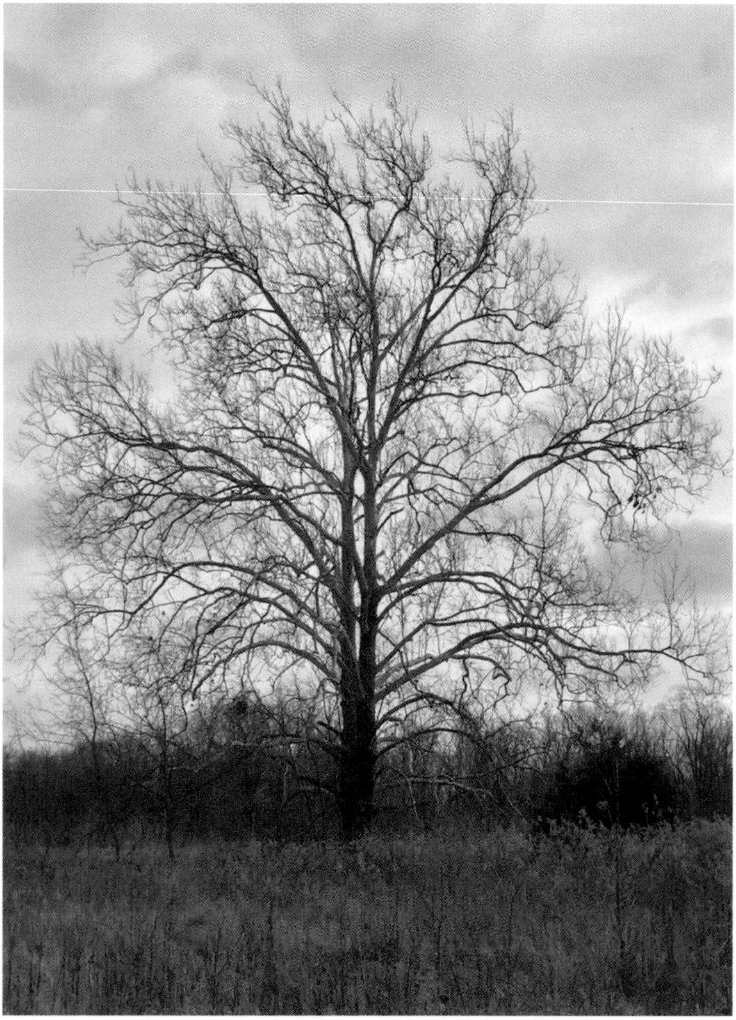

Twins

Unnoticed

Mowed around

Maybe sniffed by dogs

Why there?

No boundary line

Not shade

Just there

A random accent

Suddenly appearing

As wayward symmetry

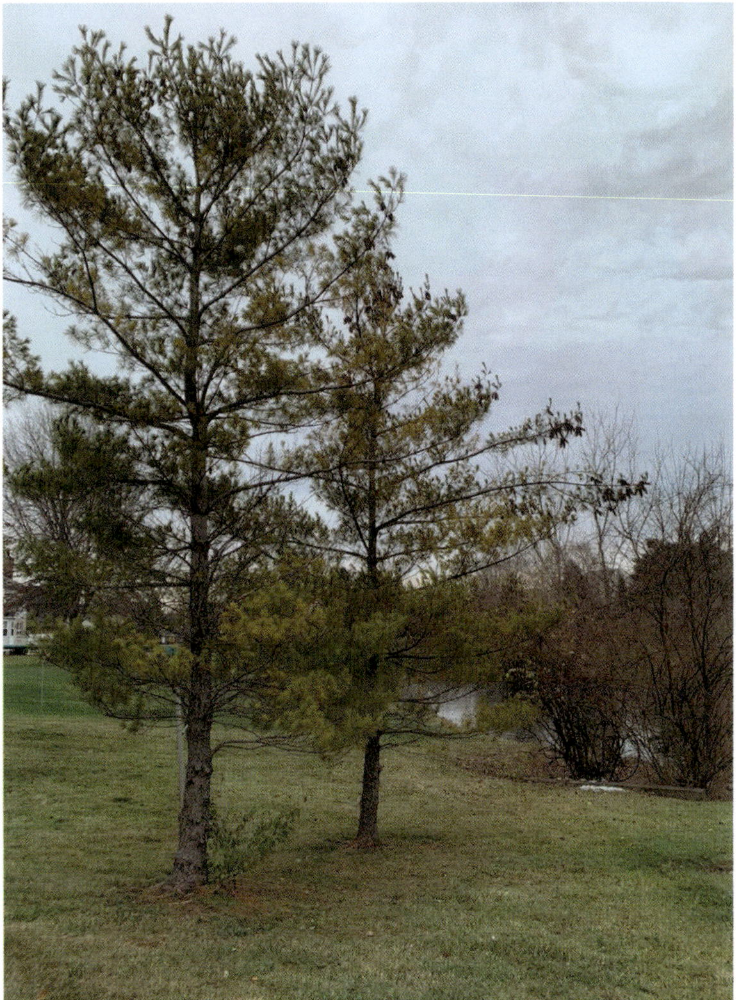

Phoenix

Annually

Fire

Death

Rebirth

When you were planted, did they know?

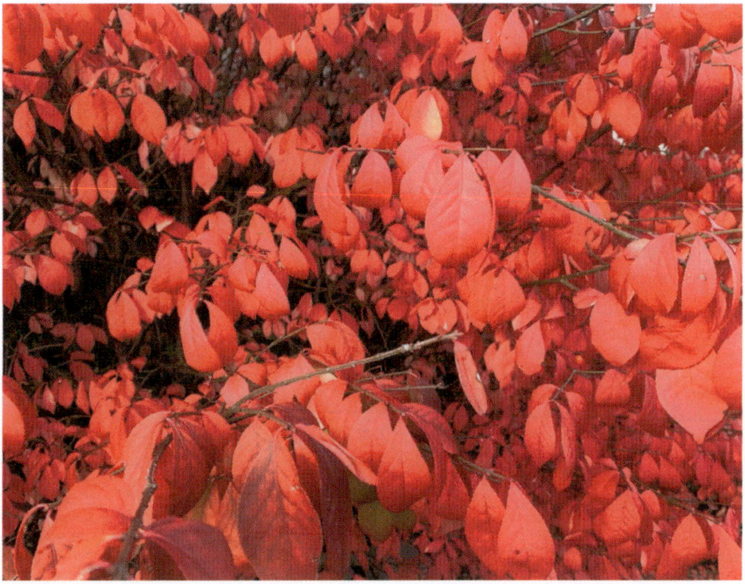

Seduction

The dress whirls

Drops from her shoulders

Into folds around her feet

Tantalizing

Graceful

Waiting

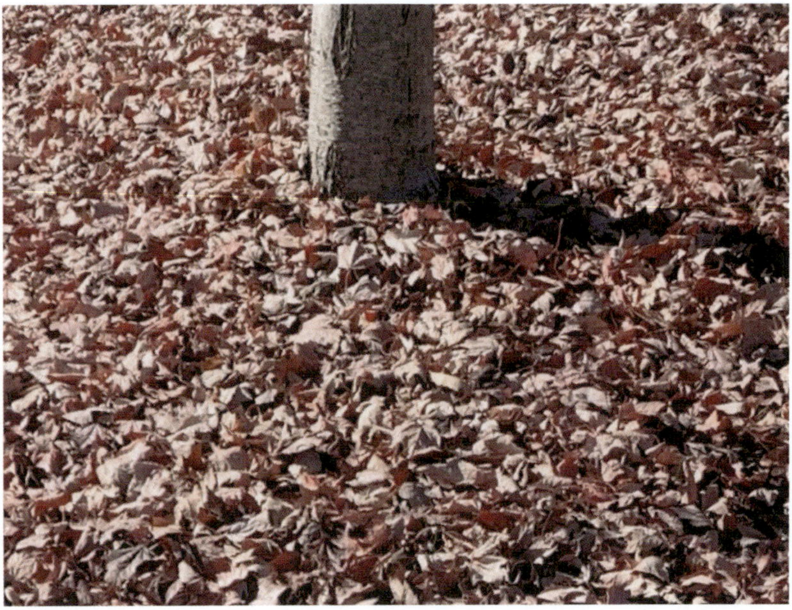

Photo Bombs

Beautiful

Interesting

Look - a line, a leaf!

I see you

Ideal, individual,

Clear

While the camera adds wires, buildings, roads

What have we lost of ourselves?

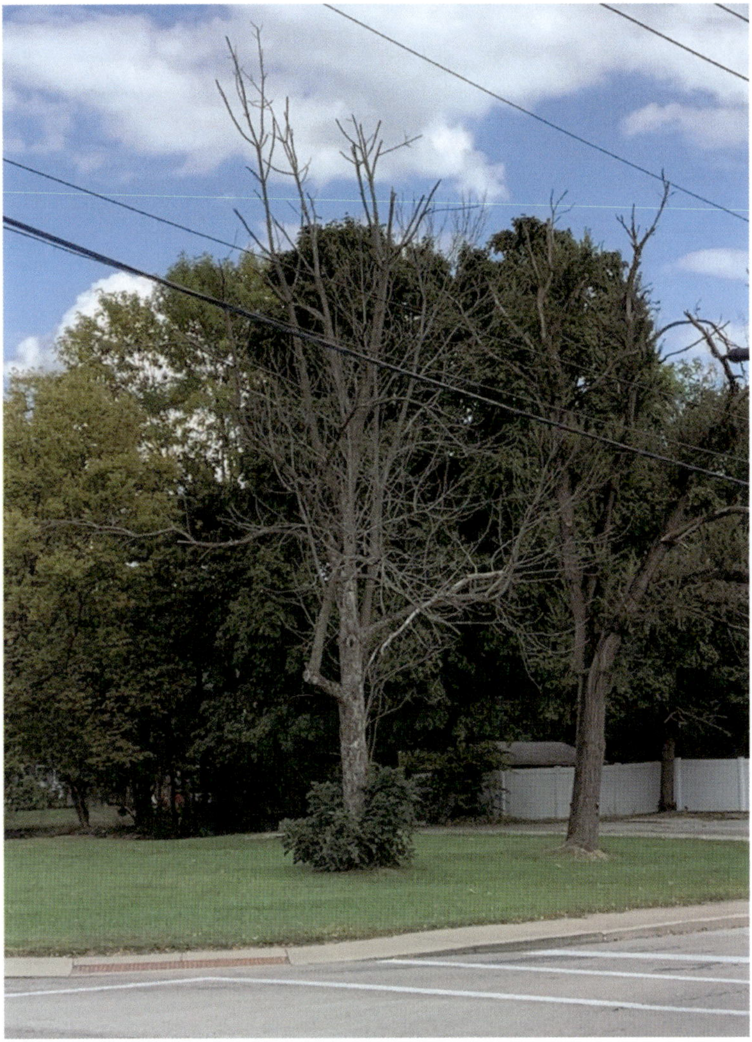

Shock

Sap

Sticky
Familiar

Wounds
Blood

An unexpected cry

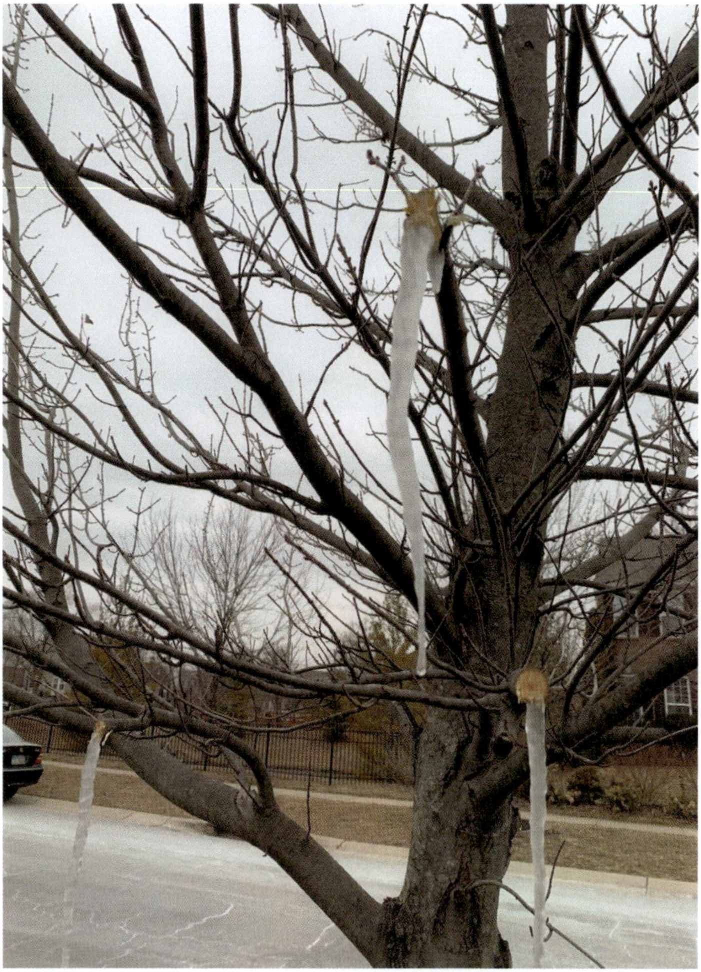

Identity

Complete

Contrast free

Not seeking to be fir
evergreen, triangular, prickly

Or redwood
majestic, definitive, ancient

Even tangled, live oak
revered, mossy

Only solo

me

here

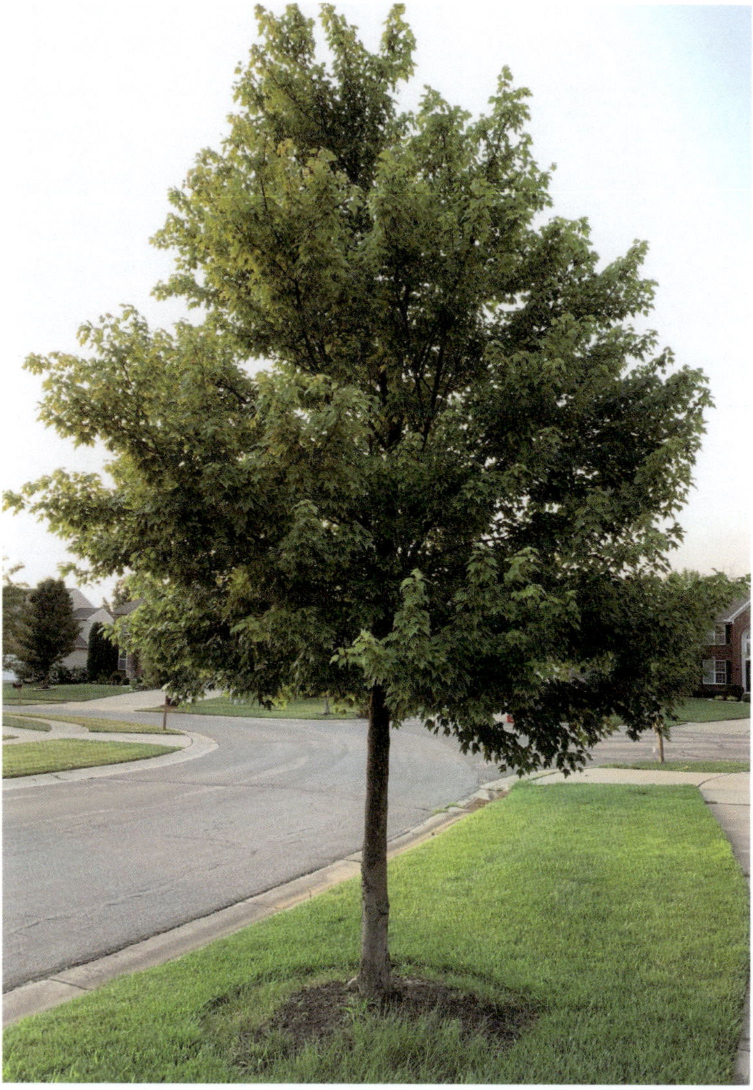

Promises

A day, a week,
  a season

Shades of white,
  hues of pink
  banishing winter
  claiming light

Defining a moment
  and my heart

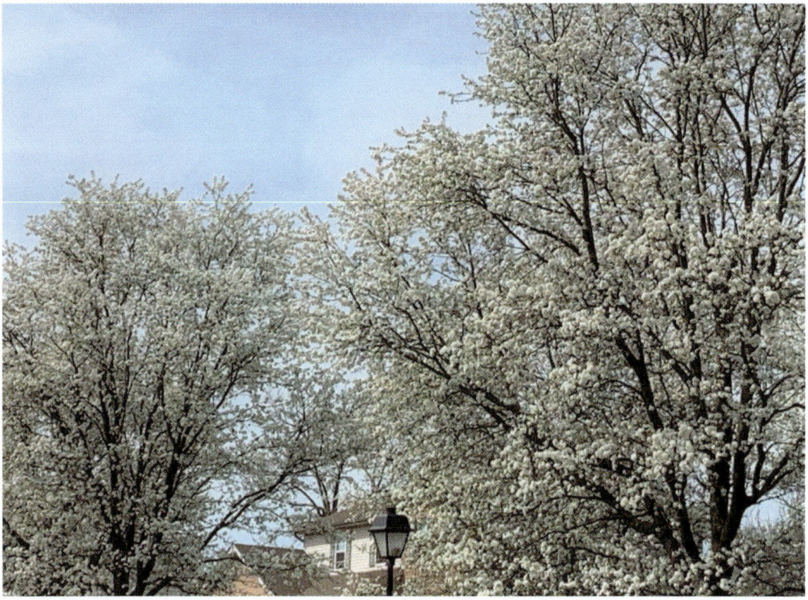

Spring Visit

I stop to greet you

Expecting buds and new growth,

Lovely! You can fly!

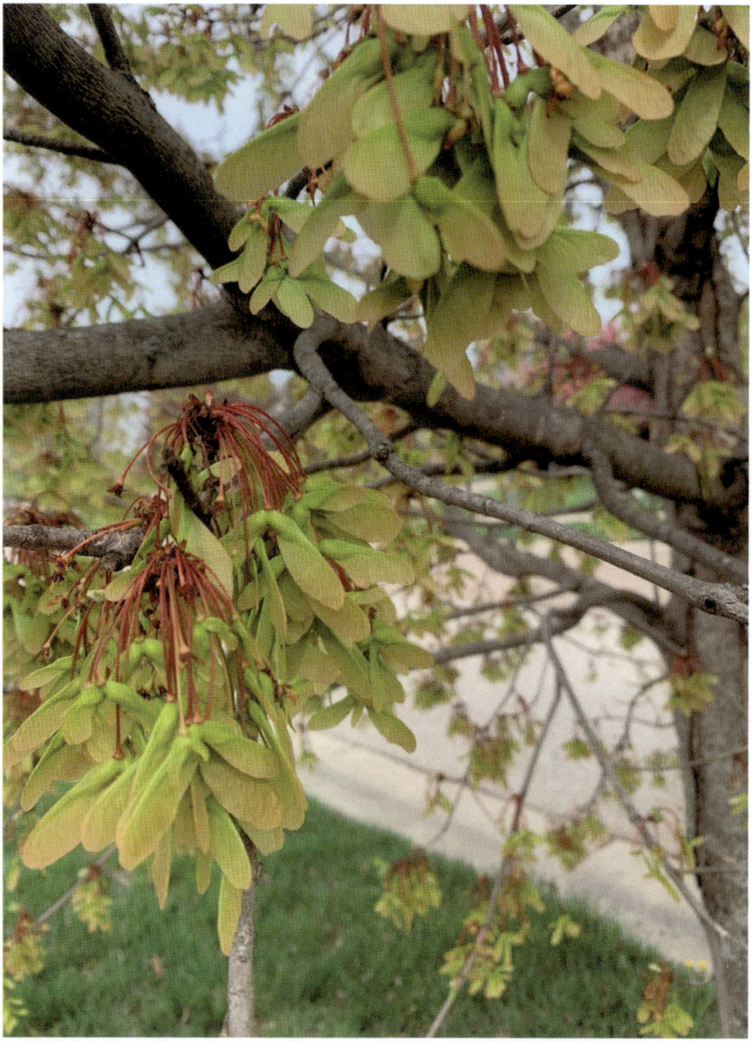

So Beautiful

So beautiful!

Take my picture–

I'll be back with a camera,
I promise

But never promised you a poem

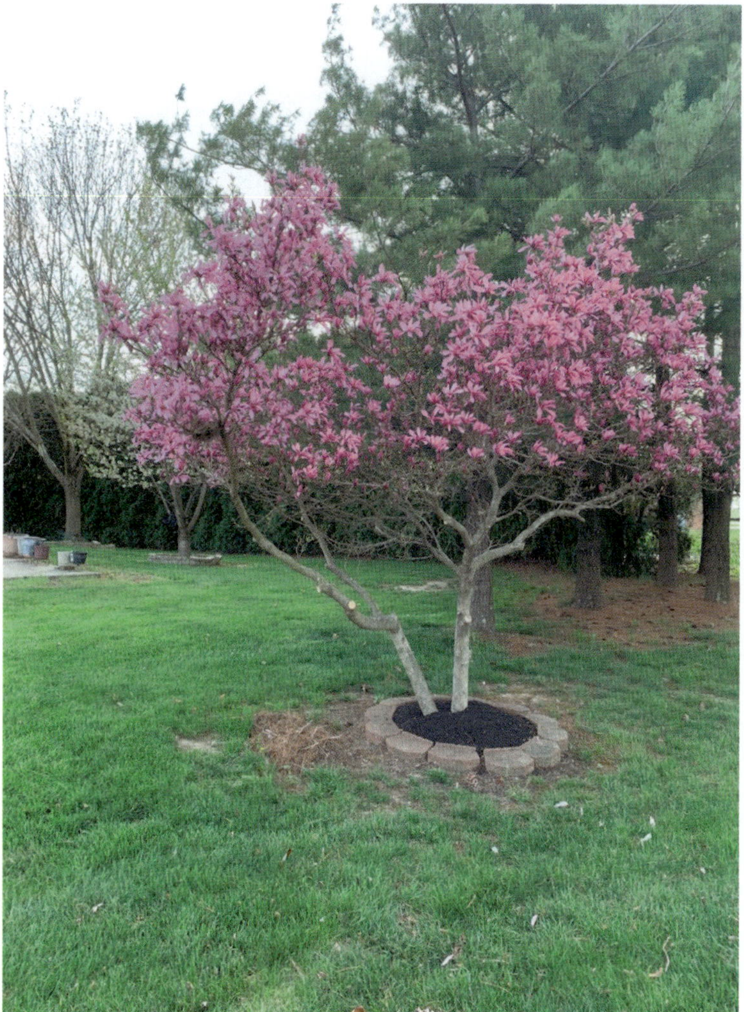

Forgotten Phone

Across the gas station concrete

One glimpse of perfect branch with almost leaves

A dare of structure, mid-Spring blessings

Lifting up heart, naming possibility

Delighting with mingled form

And no way to catch it. Except

Yesterday

Your sister tree's reflection

A mirror view

From another concrete lot

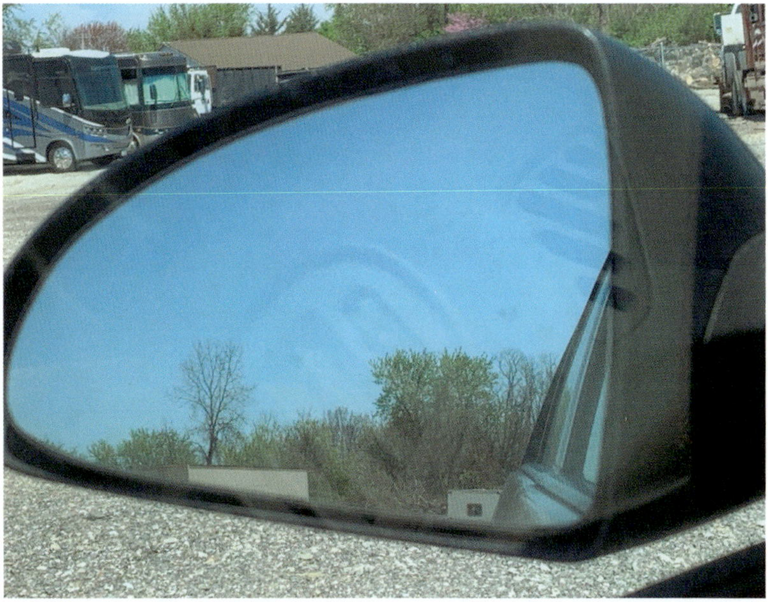

Poems
without
Pictures

April Snow

How dare it?

Heavy coats on land and bush

– and tree

Yesterday coated with emerging leaves

  tender shoots

  spring blooms

White

Driving by snow covered trees

  some are pink

Shinning through snow

The flowers won

Passing By

It's all very well to be called

See me

Love me

Touch me

Odd others can't hear

Not even video …

Whisper

  Wail

Branch and leaf

Touch

  Whirl

Untangle

  Embrace

Cameras can't catch the wind

Pictures
without
Poems

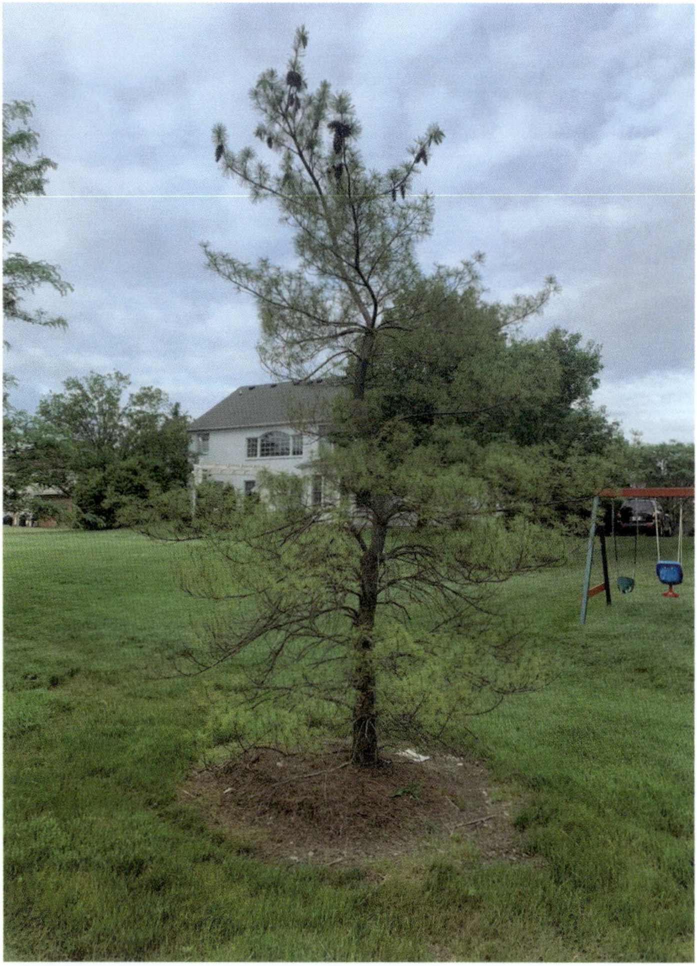

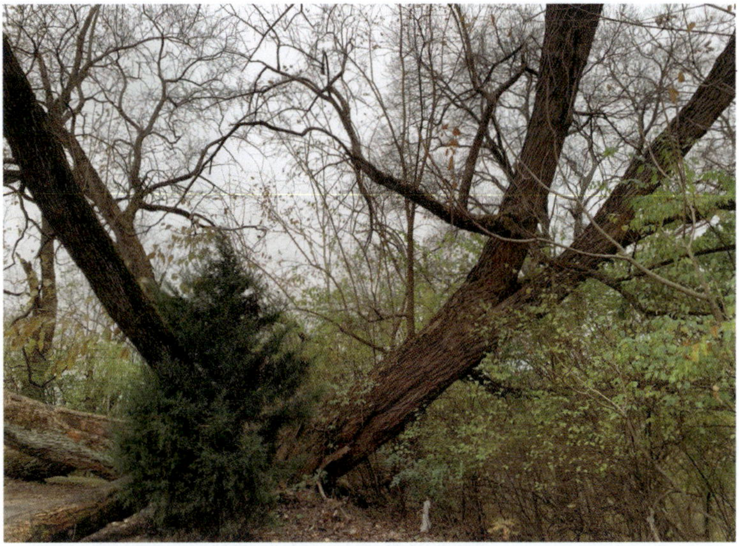

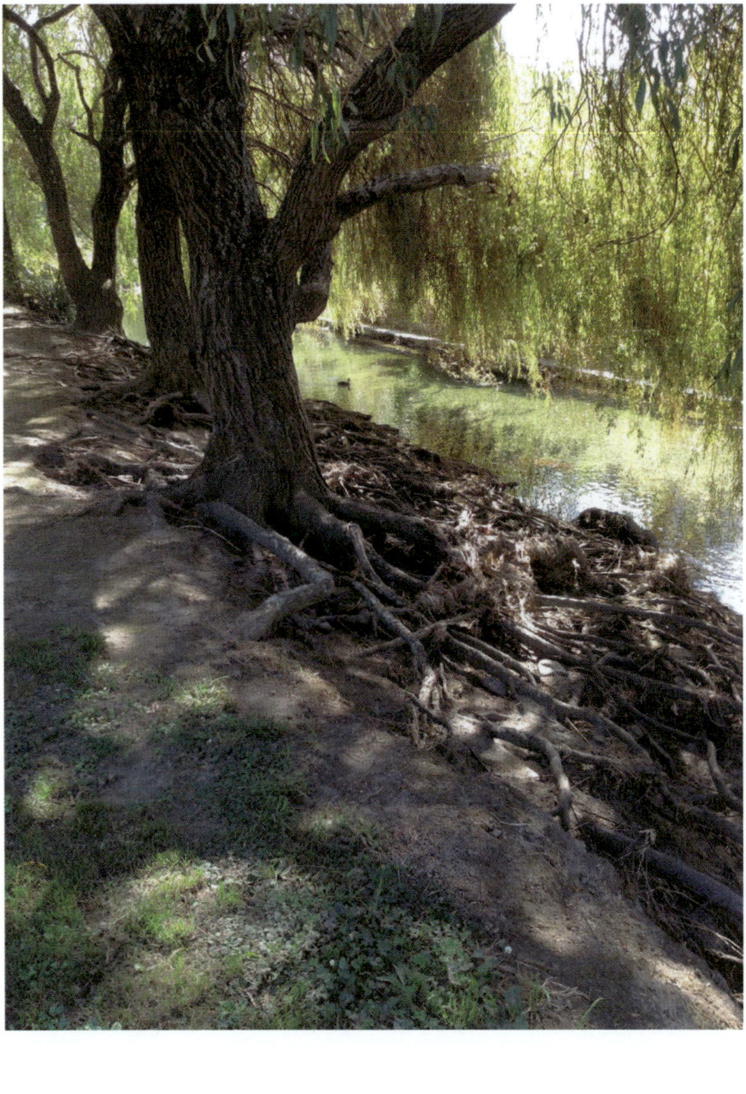

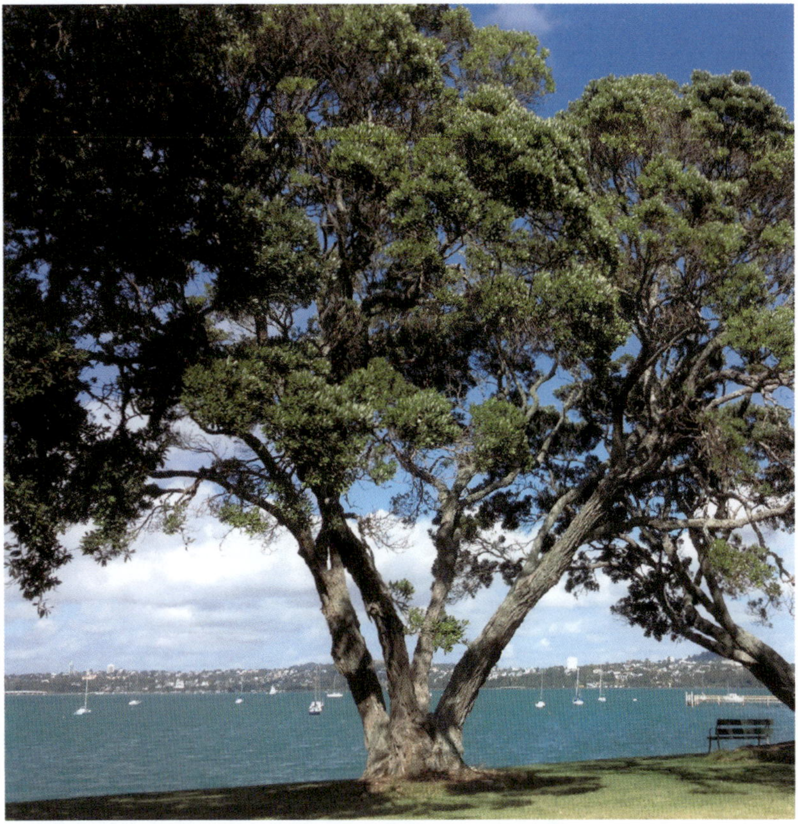

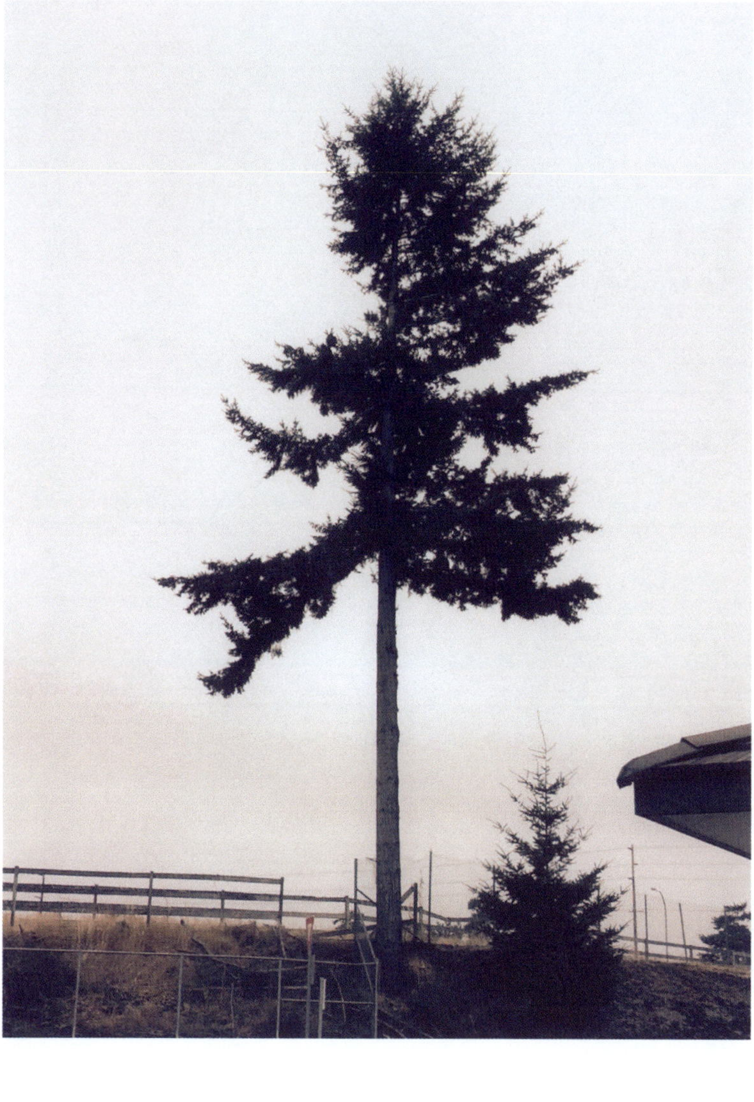

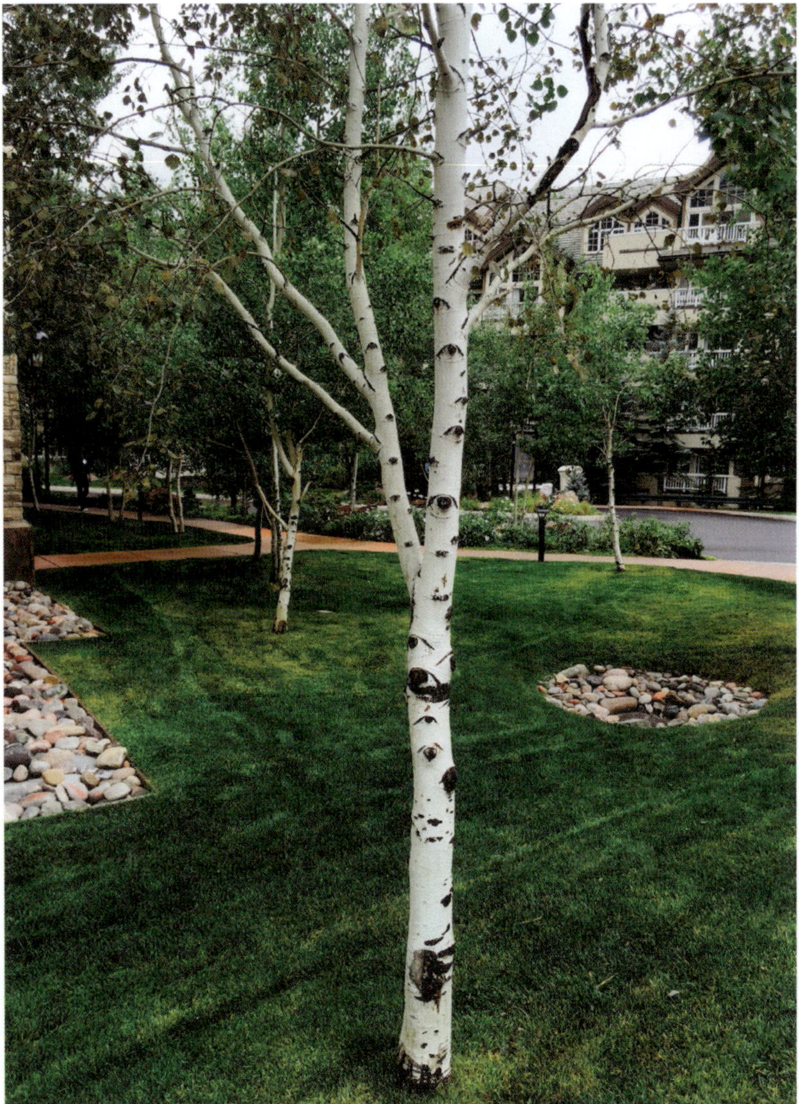

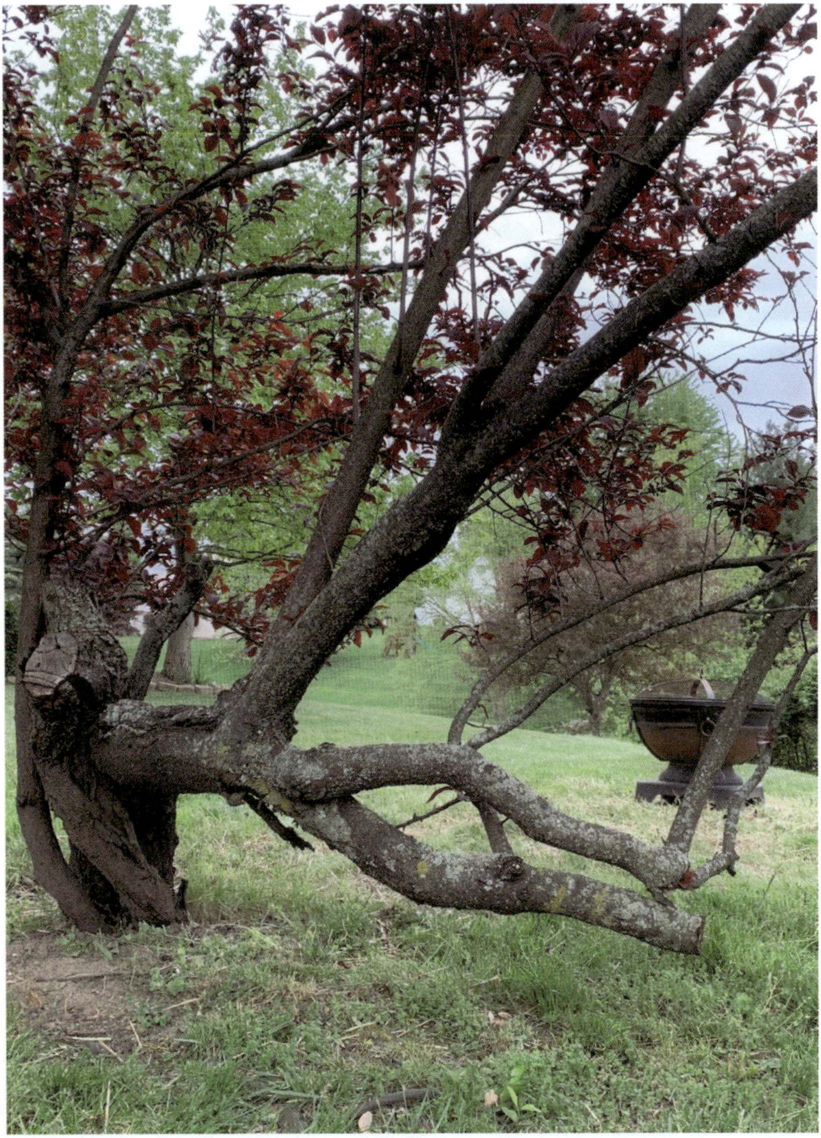

The Forest of Support

All photos are by Spirit Moxie (via an iPhone) unless otherwise noted. Notes for particular poems are: "Archetype" – art by Cynthia Jane Collins; "Connections" – photo by Lynne Hudson; "Interconnection" – photo by Kate Robinson (the card is from Herbal Healing Deck by Sarah Baldwin with Ashley Vanderkamp as the Illustrator); "Being" – photoshop work by Sarah Margree; "Skeleton or …" – photo by Matthew Collins; About the Author - photo by Harry Spirito.

None of this would have happened without the initial prompt for "The Tree Who Asked to be a Poem" from Joe Shakarchi of the Bangkok Golden Years Writing Group, which still regularly sends me emails. These days I'm supported weekly by a global writing group via Zoom which is hosted by Kathy

Kitts and includes, among others, Marcy Arlin, Jean Asselin, Dodici Azpadu, Kristen Koopman, Lynne Hudson, Susan McDevitt, Sarah Margree, Polly Ann Tausch, and Candia Thew. All have offered ongoing support, advice, and editorial wisdom. (However all errors are mine and mine alone).

– B

About the Author

B Sedgwick had her first poem published at age 7 and has been playing with words ever since. As part of that journey she studied creative writing in Alaska, taught poetry in North Dakota, and been published in such diverse places as *The Witness, Lilliput Review,* and *Five-Two Poetry.*

In 2013 she founded Spirit Moxie (www.spiritmoxie.com) where she writes Conversation posts on how we can make the world a better place. Her recent book *Moxie Moves: 10 easy ways to make a powerful difference* supports this vision. But poetry is her first love and her default writing genre at random coffee shops and bars. It is only recently that she has indulged in the phone photo craze. But sometimes poems, and trees, need photos.

Printed in Great Britain
by Amazon